AF425413

World War I, President Wilson and His Fourteen Points

History 5th Grade | Children's Military Books

Speedy Publishing LLC

40 E. Main St. #1156

Newark, DE 19711

www.speedypublishing.com

Copyright 2017

All Rights reserved. No part of this book may be reproduced or used in any way or form or by any means whether electronic or mechanical, this means that you cannot record or photocopy any material ideas or tips that are provided in this book.

In this book, we're going to talk about President Wilson's Fourteen Points during World War I. So, let's get right to it!

WHAT WAS THE FOURTEEN POINTS SPEECH?

During the last year of World War I, the 28th President of the United States, Woodrow Wilson gave a speech in front of Congress on the 18th of January 1918. Wilson hoped that the countries of the world would abide by the principles he and his committee had written to establish lasting peace in the world. He wanted this war to be the very last war on Earth. He didn't want to see a repeat of the horrors that were taking place during World War I. Millions of soldiers on both sides had been killed and the war was still raging.

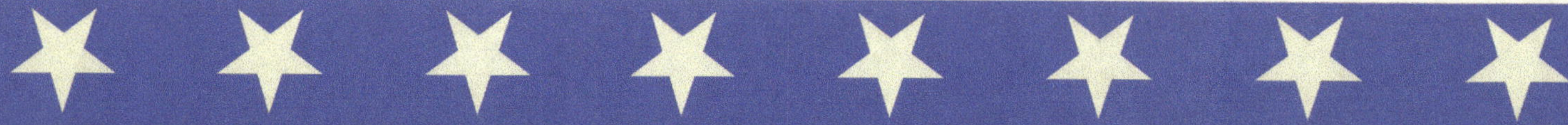

27
World War 1

Woodrow Wilson

Although the fourteen points that the President presented in this speech were not adopted exactly as written, it became the basis for many of the agreements that were signed in the Treaty of Versailles. This treaty was the official end of the war when it was signed on June 28 in the year 1919. The Fourteen Points speech also became the foundation for the Leagues of Nations, which eventually evolved into the United Nations organization that we have today. In 1919, President Wilson was awarded the Nobel Peace Prize for his contribution to ending the war and establishing peace throughout the world.

WHY DID THE UNITED STATES ENTER WORLD WAR I?

The President didn't want the United States to enter the war and the American citizens agreed. However, the United States and Britain traded with each other frequently and Germany was causing problems for their free flow of trade. Several of the ships from the United States that were due to arrive in Britain had been destroyed by mines that had been placed by Germany.

World War I Marines

Worse yet was that Germany had stated in February of 1915 that they would sink any ships whether they had civilians on board or not, if those ships were traveling around the waterways of the British Isles. A month after Germany had made this announcement to the world, they sank an American ship that was privately owned called the William P. Frye. Wilson was enraged, but the German government called the sinking an accident, so no action was taken by the U.S.

Unfortunately, this wasn't the end of it. Off the Irish coast, on May 7th of that same year, the Lusitania, an ocean ship owned by Britain was hit by German submarine torpedoes. There were almost 2,000 civilians on board and about 1200 were killed. Of those killed, there were over 120 United States citizens. Germany claimed that the ship had been carrying weapons and ammunition. The wreck of the ship remains under the water and it's still unclear as to whether the ship was truly carrying firearms or not. At this point, Wilson demanded that Germany stop these attacks on ships carrying passengers and goods.

Sinking of the Lusitania
NORMAN WILKINSON

In August of 1915, Germany stated that they would ensure that civilian passengers were safe before sinking vessels that were unarmed. However, they did not honor this pledge. Germany continued their attacks and in November of that year they destroyed an Italian ship, killing over 250 people including over 20 Americans. The citizens of the United States were beginning to see that Germany would need to be stopped.

Two years later in 1917, Germany proclaimed that they would once again sink any ships of any type that entered waters in the war-zone. That was the final straw for the United States. Once the United States stopped its diplomatic association with Germany, the German attacks on ships quickly escalated. Just hours after the U.S. severed diplomatic relations, the Germans sunk the Housatonic, which was an American ship. On April 6, 1917 armed with a $250 million dollar budget from Congress, the United States entered World War I on the side of the Allies and against Germany and the other Central Powers. By the time the war was over, in November of the following year, over 50,000 American soldiers had been killed.

President Woodrow Wilson

WRITING OF THE FOURTEEN POINTS SPEECH

President Woodrow Wilson worked with several other writers to prepare this important Fourteen Points speech.

The other writers were:

- ⇩ Walter Lippman, a well known journalist who had been a consultant to the president throughout the war

- ⇩ Edward House, a diplomat and a respected politician who had also advised the president throughout the war and led "The Inquiry"

- ⇩ A group of 150 scholars who were called "The Inquiry," which were members of a committee whose job it was to help the president prepare the materials for peace negotiations

Walter Lippmann

Portrait of Woodrow Wilson

THE GOALS OF THE FOURTEEN POINTS SPEECH

President Wilson, his other authors, and "The Inquiry" committee hoped that the Fourteen Points speech would achieve certain goals:

- To provide a roadmap for future peace on Earth
- To be used as the basis for the negotiations that would take place at the end of the war
- To influence a quick end to the conflict
- To generate interest and support for Wilson's peace plan and policies
- To prevent the reasons that led to the conflict so that it wouldn't happen again in the future

WHEN WAS THE SPEECH MADE?

The president gave this important speech in front of the U.S. Congress on the 8th of January 1918 in a joint session. The points that Wilson made in this speech were designed to create a pathway for the countries involved in the war to end the battle, respect each other's boundaries, and avoid conflicts in the future. The points he discussed were the basic tenets for an armistice that would end the war. He was the only leader throughout the conflict who had outlined the goals for the end of the war and lasting peace.

A BRIEF SUMMARY OF THE FOURTEEN POINTS

The Fourteen Points Speech isn't long. However, it contains language that is more formal than we would use today. The following list provides a summary of the intention of each of the fourteen points in the speech.

Point 1

All diplomatic discussions between nations will be open and transparent for all the world to see. There will be no secret or covert agreements between nations.

Woodrow Wilson

Point 2

The seas around the world will be free and safe to travel during both war and peace.

Point 3

Countries who agree to worldwide peace will be given the freedom to trade and exchange goods with each other.

Old World War 1 Cannon

Point 4

All countries will reduce their weapons and armies in an effort to gain a lasting peace worldwide.

Point 5

Any claims of lands that belong as colonies to other countries will be reviewed to ensure they are fair and just.

German Troops

Point 6

German troops will immediately leave Russian soil. The Russian people will have the right to choose the government they want to run their country.

Point 7

Belgium will be allowed to have its own independent government. Germany will evacuate and leave Belgium soil.

Belgium

Alsace-Lorraine

Point 8

France will get back all the territory that was lost to them in the war including the disputed region of the Alsace-Lorraine.

Point 9

All Italian populations will be part of the country of Italy and Italy's borders will be established to reflect this.

Italy

RUSSIAN
POLAND
CZECHOSLOVAKIA
Prague
Kraków
Galicia
3.10.1918
Lviv
28.10.1918
AUSTRIA
Vienna
Bratislava
zburg
11.1918
RIA
Sopron
16.11.1918
Budapest
HUNGARY
Transylvania
1.12.1918
Szeged
Ljubljana
HUNGARY
RC
Trieste
Zagreb
Temesvár
(Timişoara)
Croatia
Fiume (Rijeka)
ula
4.12.1919
STATE OF SLOVENES,
CROATS AND SERBS
Belgrade
Zara (it.)
(Zadar)
Bosnia
Sarajevo
SERBIA
BULGAR
Split
ADRIATIC
SEA
Mostar
Herzegovina
Montenegro
Sofia
BULGA
Alsace-Lorraine
ALBANIA

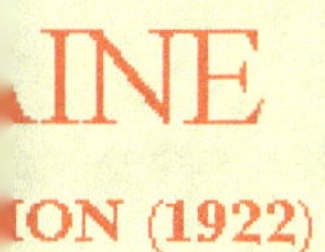

Point 10

The country of Austria-Hungary will be given the freedom to maintain an independent government.

Point 11

The Central Powers will leave the country of Serbia, the country of Montenegro, and the country of Romania. These three countries will have independence.

Montenegro

Ottoman

Point 12

People living under the rule of the Ottoman Empire will have security. The Turkish people will have their own independent country.

Point 13

The people of Poland will have an independent government and country.

Poland

League of Nations

Point 14

A special association called the League of Nations will be formed. One of its main goals will be ensure that all countries, no matter what their size, be allowed to be free and independent.

WHAT WAS THE REACTION TO WILSON'S PEACE PLAN?

Unfortunately, the other Allies didn't go along with Wilson's plan point by point. The leaders of Britain and France felt that Wilson was too much of an idealist. They didn't believe the principles he set out could ever be accomplished in a world where wars were waged and boundaries continuously debated. The leader of France at that time, Georges Clemenceau, felt that Germany must be punished severely for their role in the instigation and escalation of the war. He was very opposed to Wilson's softer "peace with no blame" strategy for dealing with Germany. He made a case for much stricter penalties for Germany. The other Allies agreed with him. The economy in France was destroyed by the Germans, so Clemenceau wanted Germany to pay for their actions.

Georges Clemenceau

Signing of the Treaty of Versailles

THE LEGACY OF THE FOURTEEN POINTS

The President's speech helped to smooth the path to get Germany into peace talks toward the end of World War I. However, when the Treaty of Versailles was created, the penalties against Germany were very severe. Germany owed the Allies a huge sum of money, about 33 billion dollars, to pay back for their role in the war.

Awesome! Now you know more about President Wilson's Fourteen Points. You can find more Military books from Baby Professor by searching the website of your favorite book retailer.

Home of President Woodrow Wilson

Visit

BABY PROFESSOR
EDUCATION KIDS

www.BabyProfessorBooks.com
to download Free Baby Professor eBooks
and view our catalog of new and exciting
Children's Books

www.ingramcontent.com/pod-product-compliance
Lightning Source LLC
Chambersburg PA
CBHW080259180726

47999CB00018B/2699